Graphic Organizers in Social Studies™

Learning About America's Industrial Growth with Graphic Organizers

Linda Wirkner

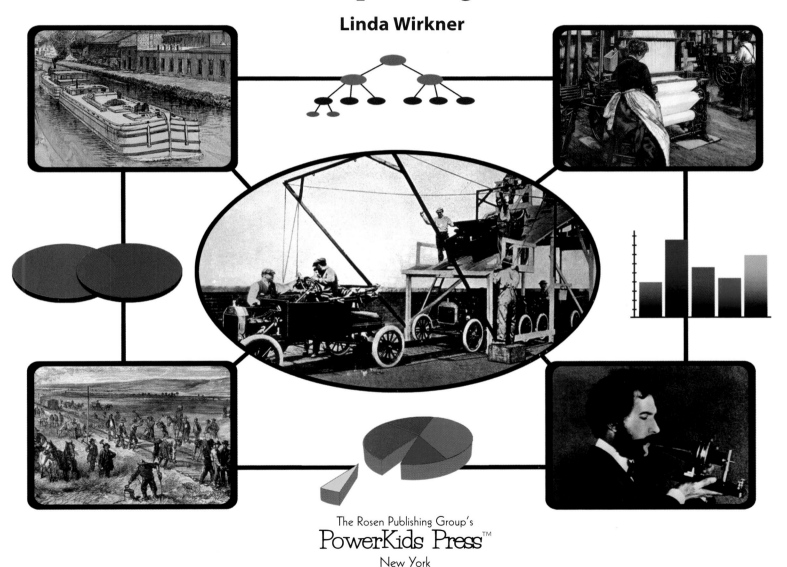

The Rosen Publishing Group's
PowerKids Press™
New York

To Millie, the best mother-in-law ever

Published in 2005 by The Rosen Publishing Group, Inc.
29 East 21st Street, New York, NY 10010

First Edition

Editor: Orli Zuravicky
Book Design: Michael Caroleo

Photo Credits: Cover and title page (middle) Library of Congress Prints and Photographs Division; cover and title page (top left, top right, bottom left), pp. 8 (bottom left and middle), 11, 15, 19 © North Wind Picture Archives; cover and title page (bottom right), pp. 8 (top right, bottom right), 16 © Bettman/Corbis; p.8 (top left) © Index Stock Imagery Inc.

Library of Congress Cataloging-in-Publication Data
Wirkner, Linda.
Learning about America's industrial growth with graphic organizers / Linda Wirkner.
     p. cm. — (Graphic organizers in social studies)
Includes bibliographical references and index.
ISBN 1-4042-2812-8 (lib. bdg.) — ISBN 1-4042-5053-0 (pbk.)
1. Industrial revolution—United States—Juvenile literature. 2. Transportation—United States—History—Juvenile literature. 3. Graphic organizers—Juvenile literature. [1. Industrial revolution. 2. Transportation—History.] I. Title.

HC105.W57 2005
338.0973'09'034—dc22
                                        2003026926

Manufactured in the United States of America

Contents

KWL Chart: Change in America

What I **K**now	What I **W**ant to know	What I've **L**earned
• Today most of the things that a person needs, such as clothing, food, tools, and many other items, can be purchased in a store.	• How did Americans get the goods that they needed before stores became so common and widespread?	• In early America, people had to make their own clothes and grow their own food. Even items like furniture and tools were made locally.
• Today items like clothing, toys, tools, books, and thousands of other things are made by machines in factories. These things are made very quickly, and many copies of the same good can be made at once.	• When were these machines first invented and built?	• The first steam engine was created in the 1700s by James Watt. This engine made it possible for machines to make goods faster than people could by hand. This is how factories began.
• Today people can travel all over the world by boat, train, bus, and airplane.	• What caused the need for these forms of transportation?	• In the 1700s, people began to move west to start farms. There was a big distance between the 13 states in the East and the territory in the West. People needed a way to get goods from one place to another, so they began building roads. Over time, people continued to discover new ways to make travel faster.

A Time of Change

In the mid-1700s, the **Industrial Revolution** began in Britain. Scotsman James Watt invented the first workable steam engine, which supplied more power and used less **fuel** than did other engines. This invention led to machines powered by steam engines, which made goods faster than anyone could by hand. By the 1800s, America was experiencing the Industrial Revolution as well. Manufacturing became a huge industry in the East. Cities grew as factories opened. America was growing, and people were moving west for better farmland. However, the lack of good **transportation** and **communication** created a gap between the eastern and western parts of the country. To connect these areas, people invented new forms of transportation and communication.

    Graphic organizers are written tools that organize facts. In this book, they will help you to learn about industrial growth.

A KWL chart can help you to study. The K stands for information you already know, which goes in the first column on the left. The W stands for what you want to know, which goes in the middle column, and the L stands for what you have learned. This KWL chart is about change in America.

The Beginning of America's Industrial Revolution

In 1790, Samuel Slater built the first steam-powered **textile mill**, in Rhode Island. Textile factories quickly opened all over the East. However, people were still separating cotton seeds from the plants by hand, which took a long time. In 1793, Eli Whitney invented the cotton gin, a steam-powered machine that removed the seeds from the plants. Then, in 1797, Whitney improved the method of **standardizing** the parts of a gun. Many parts could be made at once, and each part could fit into any gun that he made. This idea, called interchangeable parts, led to the **mass production** of goods. Machines began making large amounts of goods quickly, creating a **surplus**. To sell enough of these extra goods to make a **profit**, people needed to get them from one part of the country to the other. People realized that for this to be possible, better and faster forms of transportation were necessary.

This is a cause-and-effect chart. It lists causes on the left and effects on the right. Causes are events that happen that make other things happen. Events that happen as a result of causes are called effects. This chart explains some causes and effects that led to America's industrial revolution.

Cause-and-Effect Chart: Inventions that Led to America's Industrial Revolution

Cause

Effect

In 1790, Samuel Slater opened the first steam-powered spinning mill. The spinning machines could spin cotton into thread very quickly.

Once people realized that a machine could do the spinning for them, spinning factories appeared all over the Northeast. Cotton was spun faster then ever before. This created more cloth than was needed.

In 1793, Eli Whitney created the cotton gin. This machine separated the cotton seeds from the plant. It could remove seeds from 50 pounds (23 kg) of cotton per day.

The ability to remove cotton seeds more quickly meant that much more cotton was available for spinning. The amount of cotton could now match the need created by steam-powered spinning machines. This need for cotton helped southern farmers because most cotton was grown in the South.

In 1797, Whitney improved on the idea of interchangeable parts. This made mass production of products possible. This meant that machines could produce many copies of the same product at the same time.

Mass production of products meant that it was possible to create more of the product than was necessary for living. The extra products could be sold for a profit.

Concept Web: Colonial Transportation

Some people used wagons to get things from one place to the other. Wagons were pulled by horses or oxen. Some wagons had 4 wheels, some wagons, called carts, had only 2 wheels. Although they could carry a lot of goods, wagons were only partly covered. Bad weather, such as rain and snow, often destroyed what was being carried.

Walking was the primary, or main, method of transportation in earlier times. People generally could walk 4 miles per hour. In 10 hours, a person could walk about 40 miles (64 km).

Colonial Transportation

The upper class used carriages, which were private, fancy enclosed wagons. Carriages were not useful everywhere because they needed roads on which to travel, and there were not many roads in colonial times. In addition, people had to pay taxes to own carriages.

Oxen were also used for travel. Oxen were much slower than horses, but they were also much stronger. They could carry heavier loads and were easier to deal with than horses.

Horses were not as common in early times as one might think. They were used mostly by upper-class colonists and businessmen. They were expensive to keep because they needed to be fed and cared for in a special way. A horse can travel about 20 miles (32 km) in 24 hours.

Transportation Troubles

Traveling from one place to another on horseback was not easy in America's early days. Most roads were made of dirt. Only some roads had hard surfaces to keep the horses' hooves from sinking into the ground. In the winter, ice and snow covered the roads, making them impossible to use. In the spring, the warm weather and rain turned the dirt into mud. In those times, it took an entire day to travel a distance that today one could travel in an hour by car. In 1753, Benjamin Franklin, an important government leader, was put in charge of the colonies' postal service. He improved roads so that mail could be moved around the country more **efficiently**. He had people build corduroy roads, or roads that were made from dirt-covered logs. People began experimenting with ways to improve travel. This improvement in travel became known as the transportation revolution.

A concept web can help you to organize facts about a main idea. The main idea goes in the center of the web, and the connected facts are written around it. Concept webs also show pictures to help you understand the subject. This web is about colonial transportation.

Roads and Canals

By 1803, many Americans had moved to the West to start farms. Since it was so hard to move products from east to west, people decided to build a road to connect the two parts of the country. Construction of the National Road began in Cumberland, Maryland, in 1811. By 1850, the road reached as far as Illinois. New, flat, paved roads, like the National Road, were built all over the country. Turnpike roads had long pikes, or poles placed across the entrances. The pikes were lifted after travelers had paid a fare. Fares helped to pay for construction. People also built **canals**, such as the Erie Canal. This 360-mile (579-km) canal carried people and goods from the Hudson River in Albany, New York, to Lake Erie, near Michigan. Before it was completed in 1825, the canal cost $100 to ship 1 ton (.9 t) of grain from Buffalo to New York City. It cost only $8 using the Erie Canal.

This graphic organizer is a map. Maps show you the location of different places or where certain events took place. This map shows you the route, or path, that the National Road followed. The green dots mark all of the cities through which the National Road passed.

Map: Route of the National Road

This is a hand-colored woodcut of a steam-powered boat on the Erie Canal. The Erie Canal connected the Hudson River in the Northeast to the Great Lakes, in the Midwest. This opened up a world of new trade opportunities. Completed in October 1825, the Erie Canal cost more than $7 million to build!

11

Chart: The Erie Canal, the Transcontinental Railroad, and the National Road

	The Erie Canal	The Transcontinental Railroad	The National Road (The Cumberland Road)
Purpose	The Erie Canal was used to transport goods and people in large numbers.	The Transcontinental Railroad transported raw goods to factories in the East and manufactured goods to towns in the West.	The National Road was built to close the gap between the eastern and the western parts of the country. It helped with the country's western expansion, or growth, as well.
What It Connected	The Erie Canal connected the Great Lakes with New York City by way of the Hudson River.	The Union Pacific and the Central Pacific railroads joined tracks at Promontory, Utah, to create the Transcontinental Railroad.	The National Road started in Cumberland, Maryland, and ended in Vandalia, Illinois.
When Suggested/ By Whom	Governor DeWitt Clinton of New York finally got officials to agree in 1817 to build the canal.	Asa Whitney suggested the building of the Transcontinental Railroad in 1844.	In the late 1700s, George Washington and Thomas Jefferson suggested the creation of the National Road.
Opening Date	The Erie Canal was completed on October 25, 1825.	The Transcontinental Railroad was completed on May 10, 1869.	The National Road opened for public use around 1841.
Measurements	The Erie Canal was 363 miles (584 km) long, 40 feet (12 m) wide, and 4 feet (1.2 m) deep.	The Transcontinental Railroad was 1,776 miles (2,858 km) long.	The National Road was 800 miles (1,287 km) long.

By Rail and by Sea

In the 1820s, the English built the first steam **locomotive**. In 1830, New Yorker Peter Cooper built the *Tom Thumb*, the first American steam locomotive that could carry passengers. The locomotive could carry more goods than could any horse and wagon. This sparked the idea for a railroad. People built tracks all over the country. By 1852, the Baltimore and Ohio Railroad was completed, running from Baltimore, Maryland, to Wheeling, West Virginia. In 1869, the Union Pacific and Central Pacific railroads joined tracks, creating the first **transcontinental** railroad, running from Nebraska to California. Transporting goods across the country was finally possible. Water travel also improved. In 1807, Robert Fulton's steamboat, *Clermont*, made a successful run from New York City to Albany. The 150-mile trip took only 32 hours, compared to the usual four days.

This graphic organizer is a chart. It organizes facts about subjects that are connected to a larger idea. The kind of fact is listed in the left-hand column. This chart about the transportation revolution lists facts about the Erie Canal, the Transcontinental Railroad, and the National Road.

The Market Revolution

Before the new transportation, people depended on goods from their **regional** market. This included goods that they made themselves and those that were made locally. With the new forms of transportation, farmers in the Midwest could get corn and wheat to markets in the East by railroad and by the Erie Canal. Cotton grown in the South could be taken by railroad to New England cotton mills. Cloth and tools manufactured in the East could be sent to houses and farms all over the country. Regions began to **specialize** in the goods that they produced best. Transportation made these products available to the entire country, not just to local regions. Markets that had been regional became national. This market revolution allowed people to profit from their products. As new towns were built along train routes, new job opportunities and new national markets were created.

This is a pie chart. Pie charts show percentages, which are fractions, or parts, of 100. Each slice of the pie is a fraction of 100. This pie chart shows the percentages of people who worked in manufacturing in most of the states in 1850. Some numbers are so small they seem to be 0%.

Pie Graph: Employment in Manufacturing in 1850

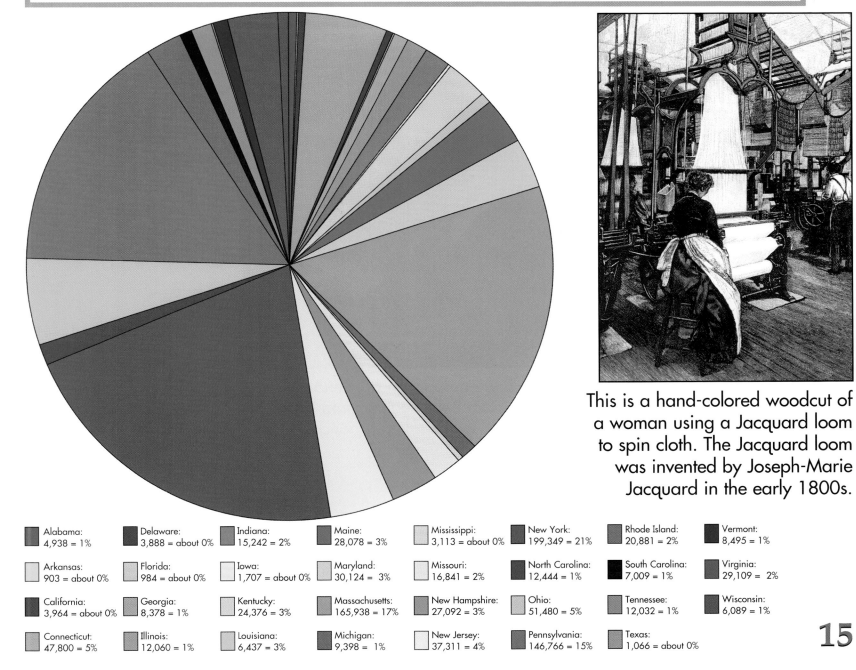

This is a hand-colored woodcut of a woman using a Jacquard loom to spin cloth. The Jacquard loom was invented by Joseph-Marie Jacquard in the early 1800s.

Alabama: 4,938 = 1%

Delaware: 3,888 = about 0%

Indiana: 15,242 = 2%

Maine: 28,078 = 3%

Mississippi: 3,113 = about 0%

New York: 199,349 = 21%

Rhode Island: 20,881 = 2%

Vermont: 8,495 = 1%

Arkansas: 903 = about 0%

Florida: 984 = about 0%

Iowa: 1,707 = about 0%

Maryland: 30,124 = 3%

Missouri: 16,841 = 2%

North Carolina: 12,444 = 1%

South Carolina: 7,009 = 1%

Virginia: 29,109 = 2%

California: 3,964 = about 0%

Georgia: 8,378 = 1%

Kentucky: 24,376 = 3%

Massachusetts: 165,938 = 17%

New Hampshire: 27,092 = 3%

Ohio: 51,480 = 5%

Tennessee: 12,032 = 1%

Wisconsin: 6,089 = 1%

Connecticut: 47,800 = 5%

Illinois: 12,060 = 1%

Louisiana: 6,437 = 3%

Michigan: 9,398 = 1%

New Jersey: 37,311 = 4%

Pennsylvania: 146,766 = 15%

Texas: 1,066 = about 0%

15

Sequence Chart: How Bell's Telephone Worked

Step 1: Bell placed a microphone at one end, inside a large metal tube. When someone spoke into the microphone, the tube vibrated, or moved back and forth.

Step 2: Under the tube was a metal cup, where there hung a metal needle. This needle was connected to a battery. The vibration from the voice made the needle vibrate.

Step 3: The needle moved up or down depending on the sounds that were being produced.

Step 4: The battery was also connected to the cup. The vibration of the needle created an electrical current.

Step 5: The receiver was made of a metal plate and a magnet. The magnet pushed and pulled on the metal plate based on the changing current.

Step 6: The plate vibrated according to the pushing and pulling of the magnet, recreating the sounds of the words that were spoken into the tube.

This is a photograph of Alexander Graham Bell speaking into his telephone. It was taken around 1876.

Inventions in Communication

In 1800, it took 20 days for a letter to get from Maine to Georgia by mail. By 1844, Samuel Morse had invented the first working **telegraph**, an electronic machine that could send codes across distances. Morse made these codes into words using an alphabet of dots and dashes that he created. Soon telegraph stations began to appear around the country. However, only one telegraph message could be sent at a time. In 1876, Alexander Graham Bell displayed his "electrical speech machine," which could **transmit** the human voice from one machine to another. This machine became the model for the telephone. The invention of the radio was based on the **technology** of both the telegraph and the telephone. The first radio transmission was sent in 1895. In 1899, the first wireless transmission traveled across the ocean from England. It was received two years later in Canada.

This graphic organizer is a sequence chart. It shows the order of certain events or steps in a process with a start and a finish. This chart shows the order of the steps that occur during the transmission of sound through Bell's telephone.

Immigration in America

The transportation, communication, and market revolutions created hundreds of new industries in America. The new industries created jobs. During the nineteenth century, **immigrants** from all over Europe flocked to America looking for work. Irish immigrants came to America after Ireland's potato crop failed. German, Polish, and Russian Jews came to America for **religious** freedom. Other Europeans immigrated because their countries were experiencing job shortages. Chinese immigrants came hoping for better wages. Many immigrants settled in New York, which soon became crowded. Immigrants played a large role in America's growth. Thousands of immigrants labored to build the railroads, roads, and canals that crossed the nation. However, this growth in population and cities forced the Native Americans living in the East to give up their land and move farther west.

Bar graphs can be used to show how something has changed over a period of time, or to compare facts. This graph compares the estimated, or guessed, number of Irish, Polish, German, and Russian immigrants who came to America from the 1800s to the early 1900s.

Bar Graph: Estimated Number of Immigrants Coming to America (1800s–early 1900s)

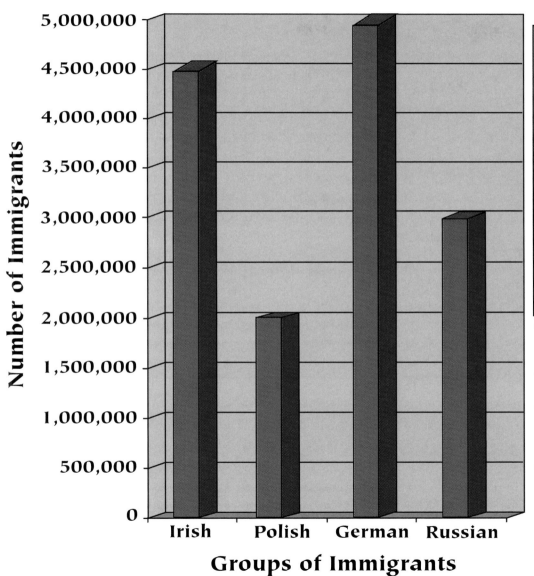

Number of Immigrants (y-axis)

5,000,000
4,500,000
4,000,000
3,500,000
3,000,000
2,500,000
2,000,000
1,500,000
1,000,000
500,000
0

Irish Polish German Russian

Groups of Immigrants (x-axis)

This hand-colored woodcut shows laborers building the Transcontinental Railroad. The work of thousands of Chinese, German, and Irish immigrants made the building of this railroad possible. They worked long, hard hours day after day for very small wages.

19

Timeline: Industrial and Transportation Revolutions in America

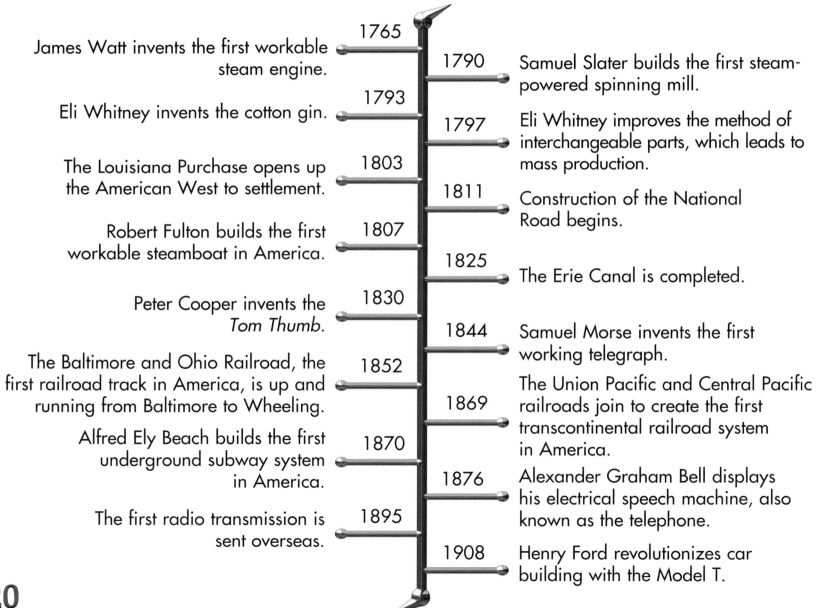

1765 — James Watt invents the first workable steam engine.

1790 — Samuel Slater builds the first steam-powered spinning mill.

1793 — Eli Whitney invents the cotton gin.

1797 — Eli Whitney improves the method of interchangeable parts, which leads to mass production.

1803 — The Louisiana Purchase opens up the American West to settlement.

1811 — Construction of the National Road begins.

1807 — Robert Fulton builds the first workable steamboat in America.

1825 — The Erie Canal is completed.

1830 — Peter Cooper invents the *Tom Thumb.*

1844 — Samuel Morse invents the first working telegraph.

1852 — The Baltimore and Ohio Railroad, the first railroad track in America, is up and running from Baltimore to Wheeling.

1869 — The Union Pacific and Central Pacific railroads join to create the first transcontinental railroad system in America.

1870 — Alfred Ely Beach builds the first underground subway system in America.

1876 — Alexander Graham Bell displays his electrical speech machine, also known as the telephone.

1895 — The first radio transmission is sent overseas.

1908 — Henry Ford revolutionizes car building with the Model T.

Twentieth-century Transportation

Over time, the steam locomotive was improved upon. By the 1900s, it became the model for the first automobile. In 1908, Henry Ford used a method of carbuilding that revolutionized the car industry. Instead of building the entire car by himself, the Model T car was built on an **assembly line**. The assembly line made it possible to produce large numbers of cars quickly. This decreased the price. For the first time, an average person could afford a car. When Alfred Ely Beach noticed New York City's crowded streets, he had an idea for an underground transportation system. He built the first underground train in 1870. By 1912, New York City had a complete subway system. Transportation continued to improve. In 1903, brothers Wilbur and Orville Wright built the first airplane. Their plane flew for only 12 seconds, but that flight changed the world forever.

This graphic organizer is a timeline. Timelines can help you to study important periods in history. This timeline shows major events in the industrial and transportation revolutions and the years in which those events happened.

A New Era

The Industrial Revolution of the 1800s laid the groundwork for modern technology. Today we live in a time when the world is run by computers. Computers control factory machines, allowing them to produce goods by the millions. Computers are also used to keep track of the **inventory** in markets all over the country. Communication from around the world is only a click away on the computer with **e-mail**. Messages that used to take weeks to arrive can now be transmitted in a matter of seconds. What began with the Wright brothers' 12 seconds of flight led to space **exploration** and people landing on the Moon. Televisions, cellular telephones, DVDs, and CDs are just a few of the technologies that we use in our daily lives. Every day the whole world is revolutionized by new technologies that continue to make transportation and communication faster and easier.

Glossary

assembly line (uh-SEM-blee LYN) A line of workers, each having a job in making a product.

canals (ka-NALZ) Human-made waterways.

communication (kuh-myoo-nih-KAY-shun) The sharing of facts or feelings.

efficiently (ih-FIH-shent-lee) Done in the quickest, best way possible.

e-mail (EE-mayl) Electronic mail sent over a computer.

exploration (ek-spluh-RAY-shun) Travel through little-known land.

fuel (FYOOL) Something used to make energy, warmth, or power.

graphic organizers (GRA-fik OR-guh-ny-zerz) Charts, graphs, and pictures that sort facts and ideas and make them clear.

immigrants (IH-muh-grints) People who move to a new country from another country.

Industrial Revolution (in-DUS-tree-ul reh-vuh-LOO-shun) A time in history beginning in the mid-1700s, when power-driven machines were first used to produce goods in large quantities.

inventory (IN-ven-tor-ee) A list of things that a person or a company has available.

locomotive (loh-kuh-MOH-tiv) The first train car, which pulls the rest of the cars.

mass production (MAS pruh-DUK-shen) Making many copies of a product at one time.

profit (PRAH-fit) To have money after all bills and expenses are paid.

regional (REEJ-nuhl) Having to do with a certain area.

religious (ree-LIH-jus) Having to do with a faith or a system of beliefs.

specialize (SPEH-shuh-lyz) To do something very well.

standardizing (STAN-der-dyz-ing) Making something an established practice or idea.

surplus (SUR-plus) An amount that is more than what is needed.

technology (tek-NAH-luh-jee) The way that something is done using special tools.

telegraph (TEH-lih-graf) A machine used to send messages through air waves using signals.

textile mill (TEK-styl MIL) A factory where cloth is made.

transcontinental (tranz-kon-tin-EN-tul) Going across a continent.

transmit (tranz-MIT) To send out a signal.

transportation (tranz-per-TAY-shun) A way of traveling from one place to another.

Index

Web Sites

Due to the changing nature of Internet links, PowerKids Press has developed an online list of Web sites related to the subject of this book. This site is updated regularly. Please use this link to access the list:
www.powerkidslinks.com/goss/amindgo/